Using smartphones in survey research: a multifunctional tool

Using smartphones in survey research: a multifunctional tool

Implementation of a time use app; a feasibility study

Nathalie Sonck and Henk Fernee

The Netherlands Institute for Social Research
The Hague, July 2013

The Netherlands Institute for Social Research | scp was established by Royal Decree of March 30, 1973 with the following terms of reference:
a   to carry out research designed to produce a coherent picture of the state of social and cultural welfare in the Netherlands and likely developments in this area;
b   to contribute to the appropriate selection of policy objectives and to provide an assessment of the advantages and disadvantages of the various means of achieving those ends;
c   to seek information on the way in which interdepartmental policy on social and cultural welfare is implemented with a view to assessing its implementation.

The work of the Netherlands Institute for Social Research focuses especially on problems coming under the responsibility of more than one Ministry. As Coordinating Minister for social and cultural welfare, the Minister for Health, Welfare and Sport is responsible for the policies pursued by the Netherlands Institute for Social Research. With regard to the main lines of such policies the Minister consults the Ministers of General Affairs; Security and Justice; the Interior and Kingdom Relations; Education, Culture and Science; Finance; Infrastructure and the Environment; Economic Affairs, Agriculture and Innovation; and Social Affairs and Employment.

© The Netherlands Institute for Social Research | scp, The Hague 2013
scp-publication 2013-22
Text editing: Julian Ross, Carlisle, uk
Figures: Mantext, Moerkapelle
Cover design: bureau Stijlzorg, Utrecht
Cover picture: Herman Zonderland, Delft

ISBN 978 90 377 0680 2
NUR 740

Distribution outside the Netherlands and Belgium: Transaction Publishers, New Brunswick (usa)

The Netherlands Institute for Social Research | scp
Rijnstraat 50
2515 xp Den Haag
The Netherlands
Tel. +31 70 340 70 00
Website: www.scp.nl
E-mail: info@scp.nl

The authors of scp publications can be contacted by e-mail via the scp website.

Contents

Summary

The introduction and rapid spread of smartphones among the Dutch population has made the innovative research domain using smartphones as a new method of data collection an increasingly important area for further investigation. The Netherlands Institute for Social Research | scp has been engaged in one of the first experiments involving the use of a smartphone app to collect time use data in combination with real-time information measured by experience sampling and auxiliary data through reality mining. For a pilot study using smartphones as a survey tool, scp worked closely with CentERdata, a research institute attached to Tilburg University. This report provides a detailed summary of a pilot study conducted in the Netherlands in 2011/12 to test the use of smartphones in carrying out time use surveys. The pilot was carried out as a feasibility study among a group of subjects not representative of the general population. As a next step, data have been collected from a representative sample of the adult Dutch population (using the liss panel) during the year 2012/13.

Acknowledgment

The authors would like to thank CentERdata, attached to Tilburg University, and in particular Annette Scherpenzeel for overall support in this project and useful comments on this paper, Maarten Streefkerk for the project management and data collection and Iggy van der Wielen for designing the app.

1   A new way of collecting survey data

The introduction of smartphones and 'apps' (applications for mobile devices) has provided many old and new functionalities which have changed the way people communicate and search for information. [1] Today, people follow the news, check train timetables and the weather, chat with friends and plan their routes whilst on the move. This study looked at ways in which this new mode of communication and use of information could be translated to the world of data collection.

Surveys conducted face-to-face, by telephone, on paper or through the Internet often require a good deal of time and effort from respondents to complete. Smartphones allow social survey data to be collected in a relatively quick and easy way. People tend to use their smartphones many times during the day to obtain short news updates, to send messages and to check social media sites. In the same way, respondents could receive short survey questions and reminder notifications using an app installed on their phone to complete a mobile questionnaire.

It is particularly interesting to study the feasibility of using smartphones as a survey tool in the Netherlands, which is characterized by a high Internet penetration rate: the percentage of 12-75 year-olds who access the internet by mobile phone increased rapidly from 28% in 2009 to 61% in 2012 (CBS Statline 2013). Figure 1.1 shows this rising trend over the years.

Figure 1.1

Percentage of persons (aged 12-75 years) in the Netherlands with overall Internet access and by mobile phone

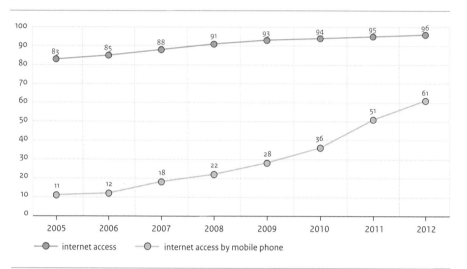

Source: CBS Statline (2013)

1.1   Time use research using smartphones

One type of survey we considered to be particularly suited to being conducted using smartphones is time use research based on completing a diary. Completing a detailed diary for one or multiple days is a burdensome activity for respondents. This makes time use research very expensive to carry out. Moreover, the relatively high commitment in terms of time and effort for respondents may negatively impact the response rates. Response rates in time use surveys are indeed generally not very high (Abraham et al. 2006, 2009; Knulst and Van den Broek 1999; Stoop 2007; Van Ingen et al. 2009; Cloïn 2013). Furthermore, if respondents do not complete the diary regularly throughout the day, recall problems may arise, resulting in less accurate time use data.

Since smartphone users have (almost) permanent access to their mobile phone, respondents can report their use of time and activities carried out several times a day, resulting in fewer recall problems. In addition, smartphones enable the collection of auxiliary data, such as GPS location or communication behaviour by mobile phone (see e.g. Raento et al. 2009). Other information can also be recorded easily using smartphones. For instance, the person's mood or short-time activities, such as (social) media usage (e.g. Twitter, text messaging, visiting social networking sites) can be reported using a 'beeping' method (Gershuny and Sullivan 1998). This method involves beeping respondents at random moments during the day with a few and short questions about their current mood (feeling happy, tired or rushed at this moment) or about the social media activities they have performed recently. The combination of data collected using a time use diary and through additional smartphone functionalities can provide a more detailed overview of the respondent's time use, behaviour and moods/well-being during the day than a traditional survey.

The Netherlands Institute for Social Research | scp has a long tradition of conducting time use surveys, being the main research institute responsible for this type of research in the Netherlands since 1975 (since when scp has sponsored time use surveys every five years). The most recent time use data were collected by Statistics Netherlands (cbs) in 2011/12, using self-completion paper diaries and capi questionnaires in accordance with the Harmonized European Time Use Survey (hetus) guidelines (Eurostat 2009). Respondents used their own words to describe their activities, side-activities and with whom they were performing these activities during a one-week period, divided up into consecutive time slots of ten minutes. After the fieldwork, the activities were manually coded into set categories by trained coders.

In order to overcome the aforementioned drawbacks of time use research, and in particular to reduce costs and increase response rates, several countries have been looking for alternative data collection methods in time use research. In Belgium, for example, the paper diary has been completely translated into an online version (Minnen et al. 2013).[2] However, if respondents fill in this online diary only once a day on their computer, it does not solve the issue of recall problems in time use surveys. By contrast, using a smartphone app would enable people to record time use at regular intervals – in those 'lost' moments spent waiting for a train, a meeting etc., or when they quickly check the news, answer their e-mails or play computer games to while away a few moments. We therefore experimented with this new data collection method using smartphones for time use research.

1.2 Study aims

In order to test whether it is feasible to conduct social survey research using smartphones and to investigate the use of the extra functionalities of mobile phones to register auxiliary data, in 2011/12 a technical pilot study was jointly conducted by scp and CentERdata. This pilot study consisted of several smartphone experiments focusing mainly on methodological aspects. Firstly, the aim was to evaluate the quality of the time use data obtained using a smartphone app. To do this, the accuracy of the time use information recorded by a mobile app was assessed by the number of episodes reported, the frequency with which people updated their diary and the general time use patterns obtained (i.e. whether they resemble similar time use research conducted using traditional survey methods). Secondly, the pilot tested how new and more detailed data can be collected which complement survey data obtained using traditional modes (such as paper, telephone, face-to-face interview). In particular, the 'beeper' method or 'Experience Sampling Method' (ESM) was used during the pilot phase to measure moods. The pilot looked at whether respondents complete such pop-up questions and how these data might provide a more accurate or detailed picture of how people felt during the day. Finally, we experimented with the collection of data by smartphones that do not require a questionnaire to be filled in or the intervention of the respondent at all. This 'reality mining' may be a key innovation in survey research, for which costs need to be reduced and response rates increased. The feasibility of collecting GPS locations and communication behaviour using log-data, which are automatically stored on smartphones and can be retrieved by an app, was therefore explored. Both are examples of auxiliary data which can provide additional information in addition to or even instead of survey questions.

Given these aims, the pilot study addressed the following three main research questions:
a   Is it feasible to conduct time use research by developing and implementing a smartphone app, and what are the effects of this method on the data quality?
b   To what extent can data collected using the 'beeper' method or Experience Sampling Method (ESM) using smartphones be employed in social research?
c   To what extent do reality mining tools on smartphones provide a more detailed overview of our social reality, and to what extent can they replace or complement existing survey methods (e.g. GPS tracker, telephone log-data)?

This report focuses in particular on the technical development of the smartphone app and the quality of the time use data obtained. In a later stage, the app was used as a survey instrument which collects data from a larger, representative section of the Dutch population (see Section 6). That will enable us to go into more methodological detail by comparing the smartphone app and paper diary methods, as well as to address more substantial research questions (about mobility, well-being, etc).

Privacy

An important issue that needs to be addressed in the new type of smartphone research is privacy. It is essential that personal data are well protected and that the privacy of participants is guaranteed. In the Netherlands, most survey research associations, such as the fieldwork agency that collected the pilot data, endorse the Code of Conduct for Research and Statistics prepared by all industry associations directly involved (see MOA, Center for Information Based Decision Making & Marketing Research).[3] In addition, the aim in the pilot was to secure voluntary participation by respondents who could drop out at any time during the study or skip certain parts of it (e.g. GPS tracking). It was also considered important that respondents should give their explicit permission for collecting auxiliary data, and that their personally identifying characteristics (such as home addresses or telephone numbers) were separated from the main data, and would not become publicly available afterwards. Privacy issues will become increasingly important in the future, especially if more information about people is collected (sometimes without even noticing it) using new means (e.g. 'big data' using Internet information), which may in turn negatively impact on the willingness to participate in smartphone studies. We will discuss this in more depth later in this report.

Notes

1   We define smartphones as mobile telephones that are programmable, and are generally characterized by a fast data connection, colour screen, camera, Internet access and location tracking (by GPS). They may have a keyboard or touch screen. This type of smart mobile phone has been in existence since 1999, but has been widely accessible to the general public since 2003 (Raento et al. 2009). In this report, the terms 'mobile phone' and 'smartphone' are used interchangeably, but refer to the 'smart' type of phones that are able to access the Internet.
2   For more information about this online time use survey, visit http://www.motus.vub.ac.be/
3   Code of Conduct for Research and Statistics (in Dutch): http://www.moaweb.nl/Gedragscodes/ gedragscode-voor-onderzoek-en-statistiek

2   Pilot design

Each new survey mode has to deal with bias related to coverage and selection problems. When the telephone mode was introduced, not everyone owned a fixed landline; and when the online mode was first used, not everyone had access to the Internet. The same is true for smartphone data collection. Since this type of survey research is rather new, selection bias remains an important problem to be dealt with, because those members of the population who do not own a smartphone will be excluded from survey data that are collected by smartphones only. Bias may occur because smartphone owners are at present still a specific group in the general population. It has for example been found that males, young persons, those living in urban areas, higher-educated people and people on higher incomes are especially likely to own a smartphone or have mobile Internet access (for Europe: Fuchs and Busse 2009; for the US: PewInternet 2013).

In order to overcome the potential selection bias, we ensured that those who did not own a smartphone could borrow one during the data collection period and hence were not excluded from participation. This also enabled us to evaluate the extent to which inexperienced smartphone users were able to use a mobile application on a device they were not familiar with. Those who owned a smartphone could participate using their own mobile phone.

Having people participate in the survey with their own smartphones poses a particular problem for software design, as different platforms (iOS, Windows, Android, Blackberry, etc.) require different methods to implement a survey on the smartphone. A possible solution would be to give respondents access to a website that is compatible for smartphones. However, at the time of the study, this method was still producing problems such as waiting for a website to load the information on the telephone screen. Moreover, the readability of online survey questions accessed by smartphone cannot be guaranteed, as the layout of a website survey on the phone screen will vary for different devices, possibly resulting in 'mode' effects (Buskirk et al. 2011; Callegaro 2010; Couper 2010; Peytchev and Hill 2010). In the future, other technologies, such as HTML5, will probably provide a stable layout across different platforms and devices (Funke 2013).

Another drawback of conducting website surveys by smartphone is that respondents need to have Internet access while completing the survey. In the Netherlands, an extensive 3G network is available for Internet connection; however, this network is not always available in buildings or remote areas. Additionally, it is also possible to access a Wifi connection (sometimes publicly available) at several locations (e.g. on some trains, cafes, etc.). However, not being permanently connected with a smartphone may cause problems in completing an online survey anywhere at any time. Finally, using a website as a basis for a smartphone survey means that auxiliary data as described above cannot automatically be collected by the phone and sent to the researcher's database.

For these reasons, we decided to develop a mobile application, or app, to be installed on a smartphone to conduct time use research. This app enables respondents to see the survey contents in exactly the same way as intended by the researcher. Furthermore, apps only have to be downloaded once in order to be accessed several times, and they also work offline, which means the respondent can fill in the diary anywhere at any time, independent of Internet accessibility. Indeed, permanent Internet access is not necessary when working with apps, as the completed survey data can be sent to the research institute automatically whenever there is a 3G or Wifi-connection (Buskirk and Andrus 2012). Furthermore, an app allows short messages to be displayed on the telephone screen, reminding the respondent to fill in the diary or asking pop-up survey questions. Finally, with an app on a mobile phone, additional data such as the person's location can be recorded by tracking GPS signals, or their communication behaviour on the phone can be collected through log-data from the telephone.

2.1 Building the app

During the development phase of the app, several decisions about the design had to be taken, which could potentially impact the response behaviour. As smartphone survey research is rather new, it is important to elaborate more on these decisions.

Following HETUS guidelines
In order to have a point of reference to compare the time use data obtained by the smartphones, we ensured that the design of the app was as similar as possible to the way in which the regular time use data are collected by the Netherlands Institute for Social Research | SCP. Thus, following the HETUS guidelines (Eurostat 2009), the time use app consisted of a diary in which participants could fill in their time use for each ten-minute interval (see Figure 2.1).

Respondents were asked to complete the time use app during two days, one weekday and one weekend day. This choice for two fieldwork days is in line with the HETUS guidelines, although in the Netherlands respondents have always completed the paper diary during seven consecutive days. Because the Dutch time use survey deviates on some points from the recommended HETUS guidelines (due to its long history in the Netherlands and hence the desire to retain trends) an overview is provided in Appendix A of the HETUS guidelines, the most recent Dutch time use survey and the smartphone app (both for the pilot study and the main survey; see Section 6).

Figure 2.1
Screenshots of the diary app: day overview of the recorded activities (left) and how to report an activity
in the app (right)

Translation of left-hand screen; Wednesday 10 July: Time & Activities: 04:00 Sleeping, 4:10 Breakfast,
04:20 Caring for and supervising children, 04:30 Paid work, 04:40 Study, course, 04:50 Gardening and
animal care, 05:00 Visiting services, 05:10 Telephoning, 05:20 Completing smartphone diary. Buttons
'Menu' and 'Complete'. Translation of right-hand screen; Wednesday 10 July at 9:30, button 'Adjust'
Your activity is: Caring for and supervising children (in your own household) + Travelling by public transport. You did this from 09:30 to 09:40. Were you alone or with someone you know? Alone: Yes / With
children up to 9 years old: No / With other family members: No / With someone else you know: No.
Buttons 'Menu', 'Copy previous activity' and 'Save'.
Source: scp/CentERdata (stbo'11/'12-pilot)

For the pilot test, two fixed days were selected to conduct the fieldwork, namely a Wednesday as weekday and a Saturday as weekend day. For the test it was considered useful to

collect data on both working and non-working days, but it was not considered necessary to have a random selection of diary days, which would be a necessary quality requirement for the main smartphone survey to be conducted subsequently among the Dutch population.

Following the HETUS guidelines, each day started at 4.00 a.m., and respondents had to complete 24 hours in ten-minute time slots. Respondents could complete the remaining time intervals of the 24-hour period until noon the next day. This allowed respondents to register time spent on sleeping and other night-time activities retrospectively, but without leaving too much time for recording activities afterwards. After completing the diary for each fieldwork day, a few evaluation questions identical to those in the traditional Dutch time use survey were asked about the specific characteristics of that day, for example whether it was a normal working day, whether the respondent was ill, on vacation, felt rushed that day, etc.

As the HETUS guidelines are mostly implemented using traditional survey methods (e.g. face-to-face interview, paper diary, etc.), they do not contain specific recommendations for innovative research methods such as the smartphone diary. Therefore, some additional decisions needed to be made for implementing the time use diary using a smartphone app.

Installing and downloading the app

In order to use an app, it first needs to be downloaded onto the mobile device. On the borrowed smartphones, the app was already installed, so that inexperienced smartphone users only needed to click on the app-button to launch the diary on the appointed fieldwork day. Respondents participating with their own smartphones could download the app before or during the first fieldwork day. Although the diary could not be completed before the appointed date, the app provided an overview of the exact fieldwork dates on which the diary should be recorded. During the initial testing phase, we found that in order to be able to download the diary app, people needed to give explicit permission on their smartphone to download apps from outside the official Android market, otherwise the app could not be installed on the phone. To resolve this issue, the app was made available for download via a link on the website of CentERdata. To install the app on the phone, respondents needed to use unique log-in information they received from the fieldwork agency in the invitation letter (see Appendix C; in Dutch).

Recording time use

There are several ways to record time spent on activities using a smartphone app, for example using a scale on which respondents can indicate particular moments, or showing a table that contains all possible time points. We decided to show respondents the starting time, which was 4.00 a.m., when the diary app was opened for the first time, or the time interval following the last recorded time period when respondents had already filled in some activities for that day. Respondents could complete their diary for consecutive ten-minute intervals following the starting time shown. It was not possible to record activities (more than ten minutes) in the future, to avoid people planning their day activities ahead, which might not necessarily correspond with what they actually did. Each completed time interval (after recording the activities performed, and with whom the respondent was at the time) could be copied for the following ten minutes. In this way, activities which lasted longer than the indicated time interval could be easily recorded. For the activities of sleeping and working, which we could expect to last much longer (around eight hours for sleeping or a regular working day), respondents could record the beginning and end time of these activities using a time wheel. This feature is often used in other apps (e.g. for planning activities in a calendar, for checking train timetables, etc.), and was therefore considered to be a functionality with which people are familiar and hence particularly suited for use in recording time and activities in the smartphone diary.

Categorising activities

Similar to the traditional time use survey, respondents could record one main activity and one side-activity for each ten-minute interval, as well as who they were with during these activities. We used the overall HETUS categories of activities but did not allow respondents to write down each activity in their own words, which would be rather cumbersome given the rather small smartphone touchscreen (or small keys to type). Instead, we used a hierarchically ranked category list with a tree structure of overall and sub-categories. Activities were listed underneath each other, which resulted in the most obvious and clear overview of the possible activities for respondents to choose from. Especially on smartphones with touchscreens, this method makes it very easy to 'tick' the appropriate activities.

More specifically, respondents could select their activities from a list of 41 predetermined hierarchically ranked categories (see Appendix B). Although these pre-coded categories deviate from the HETUS guidelines, which recommend open categories described by the respondents themselves (to be coded afterwards by trained coders), the list of activities did take into account the overall HETUS categories. If people doubted whether their activity matched one of the predetermined categories, they could find additional explanation and examples by using an information button that was linked to the activity categories. Otherwise, there was always the opportunity to type their activity in their own words, which was then coded afterwards by the researcher into the most appropriate category.

The app provided a day overview in which respondents could access a list of the recorded activities up to that moment. By clicking on time intervals in this overview, respondents were able to change (side-)activities or add new ones.

To label the activity categories, we opted for verbatim/words rather than pictograms. Although pictograms (e.g. an image of a bed for sleeping, a computer for working, etc.) could have added value in smartphone research compared to paper diaries as regards usability and the general 'look and feel' of the survey, a disadvantage of images is that they might influence response behaviour. For example, people might be confused if a pictogram of a computer is used to represent working, if they do manual labour, or if a shower is used as pictogram for personal care, while this category also comprises things such as brushing teeth and going to the toilet. Research is lacking about the potential impact of pictograms in survey questionnaires. However, it is important to test the relationships between pictograms and words extensively, in order to be able to use them in future research on digital devices. In our study, the aim was to keep activities as similar as possible to the traditional time use survey following the HETUS guidelines. Therefore, words were used rather than pictograms to denominate the activity categories.

Synchronizing data

The use of digital devices to collect survey data (computers, laptops, tablets, smartphones, etc.) requires data synchronization. This means that the information which is stored in a database on the respondent's device needs to be periodically sent to the researcher's database. One option is to have respondents manually send completed information to the researchers, for example by occasionally clicking a synchronization button. However, a drawback of this method is that researchers are entirely dependent upon what information respondents synchronize and when/how often. Moreover, this would probably require additional notifications to remind respondents about the data synchronization. It was therefore decided to synchronize the data automatically, each time there was Internet connectivity (e.g. through Wifi). In this way, times and activities recorded in the diary app were regularly sent to the main database without further action being required by the respondents.

2.2 Reality mining

In addition to implementing a diary app for time use research, the smartphone mode enables researchers to collect a wide range of complementary or auxiliary data for which respondents do not need to take any action. More specifically, information can be obtained about behaviours that could not be observed otherwise or would be biased by self-reports (Raento et al. 2009). Recording information without surveying respondents is also called 'reality mining'. This has been defined as the collection of machine-sensed environmental data pertaining to human social behaviour. In practice this means direct measurement of social behaviour through technology implemented on mobile devices, such as smartphones. For example a GPS tracking function on a smartphone enables researchers to see exactly where participants are and how they travel throughout the day. A study that compared a travel diary and GPS tracking found that respondents under-report travel distance and over-report travel times (Stopher et al. 2007). Most studies tracking GPS locations use separate devices which people need to carry with them (e.g. Stopher et al. 2007; Bullock et al. 2003; Bohte 2010; Yen et al. 2013). However, standard apps on smartphones make this functionality more generally accessible for use in research. In this way, a questionnaire about a person's mobility throughout the day could be replaced by a GPS function on a smartphone. Consequently, location data can be collected much more quickly and possibly also more accurately than when respondents need to rely on their memory.

Other behaviour that can easily be collected through a smartphone is when and for how long respondents made calls or sent text messages (SMS). It is not the content of the conversations that is relevant, but metadata about the communication behaviour can be recorded from log-data which are stored on the mobile phone (Raento et al. 2009). Additionally, it would have been possible to log the volume of data (e.g. number of MBs) used by the smartphone, but this would say nothing about which websites were visited. For example, Bouwman et al. (2013) experimented with data collected using log-information regarding the frequency and time spent on apps, website behaviour and Internet connections. However, the data obtained are very complex, as all web pages visited need to be classified. We therefore did not include this possibility in our study.

In the pilot study, we experimented with two reality mining possibilities, namely GPS tracking and logging communication behaviour. For the information about location, we decided not to record the GPS location continuously for each respondent as this would require a lot of battery power. Neither did we want respondents to send their GPS location manually at particular time points, as we considered it more accurate if a method was used that collected the GPS coordinates automatically. Therefore, we registered the location of respondents every ten minutes and/or on every movement of at least ten metres when the time use app was active. To obtain information on communication behaviour, log-data of the calls and text messages on the phone were recorded. For technical reasons, this was only possible for the Android phones, not for iPhones. Furthermore, this was only relevant for tracking people's own smartphones (not the borrowed ones), as this would correspond to people's common communication behaviour.

An important issue in relation to the reality mining approach to data collection is privacy. In our study, respondents had to give permission for the collection of auxiliary data (i.e. GPS location and communication behaviour) when downloading the app onto their smartphone. For those who borrowed a smartphone, the app was already installed, but they could always decide to turn off the GPS tracker.

2.3   Experience sampling

Time use information as recorded in a paper diary – even in ten-minute slots – can only provide a glimpse of what people are actually doing during a whole day. Short-time activities (i.e. checking an incoming message, having a chat at the coffee machine) will probably be underreported. Such information could possibly be collected in a more accurate way by sending people several invitations a day to report what they are doing at that particular moment (or during a limited time period in the past, such as in the past hour). This is very similar to data collection using the beeper method (Gershuny and Sullivan 1998). In the original beeper method, respondents, prompted by the sound of a radio device, recorded at random moments what they were doing and how they felt. This method provides a different picture of time use from the diary method. It does not give an overview of individual time use patterns or the frequency of activities of individuals, but it can be used to measure the general participation in specific activities during the day (e.g. at 12.30 p.m. about half the Dutch population are having lunch).

Apart from measuring time use, the beeper method can also provide information on behaviour or experiences that are difficult to capture with traditional survey questionnaires. For example, social media are increasingly used briefly at several moments during the day (such as sending a Tweet or checking the latest status on a profile website such as Facebook). Regularly asking short pop-up questions about these activities might therefore provide a more detailed overview of social media use throughout the day than merely using a diary which focuses on activities that are recorded in ten-minute time slots.

Moods and feelings of time pressure may also fluctuate throughout the day. Asking respondents to record how happy, sad, stressed or irritable they feel during each activity in the diary would definitely make them feel tired, irritable and rushed. On the other hand, scoring moods at the end of the day when completing the diary does not reflect mood swings during the day. Asking respondents to report such feelings in response to several random beeps throughout the day might therefore strike the best balance between respondent burden and obtaining an accurate picture.

Measuring moods using a beeper method resembles the Experience Sampling Method (ESM), developed by Larson and Csikszentmihalyi (1983) in which participants were asked at certain times to make notes about their feelings and experiences in real time. Kahnemann et al. (2004) argue that ESM is better suited to provide information on well-being than traditional survey methods, which mostly rely on recalling feelings retrospectively. Earlier studies have combined ESM with time use data, but these mostly relied on the Day Reconstruction Method (DRM) (Kahneman and Krueger 2006) in which respondents have to recall which activities they performed during the (for example previous) day. This method produces less accurate time use data than the diary method in which respondents record their activities in ten minute-intervals. The combination of ESM and the diary method is therefore believed to provide a more detailed overview of people's activities and feelings compared to the combination of ESM and DRM used in previous research.

Whereas respondents in earlier studies received a beep in which they were asked to respond several times a day (see e.g. Larson and Richards 1994), the current technology of smartphones and mobile apps makes it possible to contact respondents through notifications and pop-up questions on the phone screen (Killingsworth and Gilbert 2010). An example of such data collection is the Mappiness research project at the London School of Economics which aims to map happiness. [1] For this project, an app was designed that could be freely downloaded from their website on (only) iPhones. As everyone can participate voluntarily in the research, the results are not representative for a pre-defined population. In this particular study, respondents report their moods after being prompted (by notifications) and also unprompted (as often as they wish). Participants can even send accompanying pictures of their current situation.

During our pilot study, we implemented the beeper/ESM method to collect information on moods. More specifically, we experimented with three short questions that resembled the Mappiness study using smartphones: how happy, rushed and tired respondents felt at several moments during the fieldwork day (see Figure 2.2). These questions were designed in such a way that they fitted on one screen and could be answered very quickly, without thinking too much about it. Respondents were 'beeped' with these pop-up questions at seven random moments within reasonable time limits during the day (for example not at 3.00 a.m.). These short questions popped up at the beginning of a ten-minute time interval and could be answered only during those ten minutes. After that time interval had expired, the question disappeared from the screen and could not be answered any more. In this way, it was ensured that (more or less) real-time feelings were measured and no long recall was necessary. Moreover, the use of these ten-minute intervals for the ESM questions also ensured that the results could be linked to the activities performed during that particular time interval, with whom and at what location, as recorded in the diary.

Figure 2.2

Screenshot from the ESM pop-up questions about moods

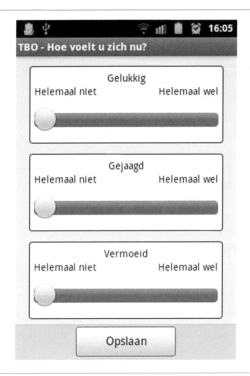

Translation of screen: Time Use Survey - How do you feel at this moment? Happy, Rushed, Tired. Not at all – Extremely. Button 'Save'.

Note: the slider remained grey if no response was given (answer was missing) and turned to colour when people tapped their response on this scale

Source: SCP/CentERdata (STBO'11/'12-pilot)

Additionally, in a similar way to the traditional Dutch time use survey, at the end of each fieldwork day respondents were asked how rushed they had felt during that day. In this way, the numerous short ESM questions asked throughout the day could be compared with the overall survey questions which respondents completed at the end of each field-work day (or at the latest, the day after).

The ESM method can also be used to measure social media use. Our aim is to use the same kind of short pop-up questions to ask about recent social media activities performed (e.g. how many Tweets someone has sent during the past hour or how many times they checked updates on their Facebook profile). As these social media activities mostly last less than the ten-minute intervals used in the diary app, these additional pop-up questions at random moments during the day may provide more accurate information about actual social media use than simple survey questions which ask for general estimations of time spent on these activities. During the technical pilot phase, we tested the feasibility of this kind of survey method using smartphones to measure moods, but not yet for the social media use. This was however implemented in the main survey that followed the pilot study (see Section 6).

Note

1   For more information on Mappiness, see: http://www.mappiness.org.uk/ or for other examples see http://www.trackyourhappiness.org and http://www.moodpanda.com

3   Data collection / fieldwork information

The app and the feasibility of completing the time use survey using a smartphone were evaluated in a series of tests. A demo-version of the time use app focused on the diary and was first designed for the Android operating system for smartphones. In October 2011, this demo-version was tested in depth by researchers from both CentERdata and scp on their own smartphones and on a similar Android-based phone that would be provided to the respondents (Samsung Galaxy Gio). It was important that the device should be technically stable and user-friendly. In a later stage, the app was also designed for iPhone devices (iOS-based). Apple imposed strict layout criteria for the design of this app, before making the app accessible to iPhone users through the Apple App Store, which was necessary for users to be able to download the app. The app was specifically built for Android and iOS devices because these were the most frequently used by the members of the LISS panel, which is representative of the Dutch adult public.[1] Blackberries, which also have a fairly high penetration among the population, were excluded from this study since they operate in a very different way from most other devices, usually have no touch screen and the screen is smaller.

In order to test the time use app among a group of actual respondents, a sample of 150 subjects was selected from the TNS-Nipo base panel, which is a non-probability online access panel.
Initially, 50 panel members who owned an Android smartphone were selected, and 50 panel members without a smartphone who were able to temporarily borrow an Android-phone provided by CentERdata. In a first wave in November 2011, this group of subjects tested the diary and its functionalities (Pilot 1). In March 2012, the same group of subjects participated in a second wave, for which the Experience Sampling Method was additionally implemented (i.e. respondents were 'beeped' at several moments during the day; Pilot 2). They subsequently participated in a third wave to test the final version of the diary app andESM questions (Pilot 3). In that wave, the log-data of people's communication behaviour were also experimentally collected (on respondents' own Android smartphones). Finally, in a later stage an additional 50 panel members were selected who owned an iPhone. They tested the diary and ESM questions in the iOS-based environment (Pilot 4).
For the selection of the three groups of subjects (50 persons without a smartphone, 50 with an Android phone and 50 with an iPhone), the aim was to obtain comparable distributions of the background variables age, gender, and education. In this way, the groups could be compared based on their data quality regardless of the background characteristics of the different groups selected. Table 3.1 presents an overview of all the fieldwork days for the four pilot tests and the groups that were involved. In order to obtain sufficiently high response rates in the successive pilot waves, it was ensured that respondents

who did not participate on the first fieldwork day were given an opportunity to participate on the same weekday (Wednesday) shortly after the first fieldwork day.

Table 3.1

Dates of the pilots

	Pilot 1 (Android users and non-users)	Pilot 2 (Android users and non-users)	Pilot 3 (Android users and non-users)	Pilot 4 (own iPhone)
Day 1	Wednesday 23 November 2011	Wednesday 7 March 2012	Wednesday 16 May 2012	Wednesday 27 June 2012
Day 2	Saturday 26 November 2011	Saturday 10 March 2012	Saturday 19 May 2012	Saturday 30 June 2012
Repeat day	N/A	Wednesday 28 March 2012	Wednesday 23 May 2012	Wednesday 4 July 2012

Source: scp/CentERdata(stbo'11/'12-pilot)

The participants received an introductory letter about the study (see Appendix C; in Dutch), a written manual on how the app works and a list of all the activity categories (see Appendix B). In addition to the written manual, participants could watch an introductory film on YouTube explaining how to use the app (and how to use the smartphone for those who had borrowed one). In addition, during the fieldwork period a helpdesk was available to answer (technical) queries. This helpdesk could be called from within the time use app if problems arose while completing the diary, but the helpdesk telephone number and e-mail address were also provided in the invitation letter.

People participating with their own smartphone (Android or iPhone) could download the app via a link on the CentERdata website (details were included in the invitation letter), while for participants with a borrowed phone the app was already installed. Before downloading, participants could indicate whether they wanted their GPS location to be tracked by the app. The GPS tracking system could also be turned off at any time after downloading the app. This had no further consequences for participating in the research (except that their locations were not stored). The GPS recorded the location for every ten-minute interval, and also whenever the respondent moved more than ten metres. If there was no GPS coverage, the location was determined by telephone location tracking.

To increase response rates, both reminders and incentives were used during the fieldwork period of the pilot. If no activities were recorded in the smartphone diary for two hours, a notification was sent to respondents to remind them about completing the diary up to the most recent activity. Subjects also collected loyalty points from the TNS Nipo panel as an incentive.

After the first tests (i.e. two days of fieldwork) a more detailed evaluation questionnaire was sent to the participants and ten qualitative in-depth interviews were held among them, to learn more about the experiences and difficulties while actually using the app. The following sections provide more information about the groups of participants selected in the subsequent stages and their responses.

Pilot 1

In the first pilot test, of the 100 panel members who agreed to participate in the time use study, 45 people participated with their own Android smartphone and 47 persons participated with the Android-based smartphone provided by CentERdata. People were asked to fill in the time use app on a weekday (Wednesday) and a weekend day (Saturday) for the entire 24 hours (following the HETUS guidelines, in which a day starts at 4.00 a.m.) (see Table 3.1 for the fieldwork dates).

The demographics do not show significant differences between the Android smartphone owners and inexperienced users (Table 3.2). For this pilot study, with mainly experimental aims, it is not important whether these groups are representative of the Dutch population, but it is important that the groups are mutually comparable so that their data quality can be assessed regardless of their background characteristics.

Table 3.3 shows the responses for both groups. It is interesting to note the low number of completes for inexperienced users on the first fieldwork day. After this first day, all the participants who did not have a complete day received a reminder call, which helped in boosting the number of completes for the second day. Overall, it can be seen that not all respondents recorded time data for the entire day, or data were not saved correctly. In total, 83 respondents completed a minimum of 75% of all time intervals for one day. Of these, 43 used their own phone, 37 a borrowed one and for three respondents it was unknown which phone they used.

Table 3.2

Demographics for both groups of participants in Pilot 1 (November 2011)

	Smartphone owners (Android)	Inexperienced users	Total
Gender: Male	21	12	33
Female	22	25	47
Age	45.8 years	43.8 years	44.2 years
Education: high	9	14	23
middle	26	17	43
low	7	6	13

Source: SCP/CentERdata(STBO'11/'12-pilot)

Table 3.3

Response numbers of Pilot 1 (November 2011)

Day 1: Wednesday	Smartphone owners (Android)	Inexperienced users
Complete	40	27
Partially complete	2	15
No observations	3	7
Never logged in	5	1
Day 2: Saturday		
Complete	37	46
Partially complete	9	1
No observations	3	0
Never logged in	1	3

Source: scp/CentERdata(stbo'11/'12-pilot)

Pilots 2 & 3

For the second pilot test in March 2012, the same respondents were again asked to participate on a weekday (Wednesday) and a weekend day (Saturday) using their smartphone or the borrowed one. A slightly updated version of the time use app was tested, and an important new feature implemented in the second test wave was the ESM to measure moods during the day. For this, respondents received seven notifications on the smartphone with short experience questions: How do you feel - happy, rushed, tired? A response scale (slider) was used for each of these moods, ranging from 'Not at all' to 'Extremely' (see Figure 2.2 for a screenshot). These notifications were sent at random moments during the day, taking into consideration reasonable time limits between which people would be able to respond, namely between 8.00 a.m. and 10.00 p.m. The notifications popped up on the smartphone screen only at the beginning of a ten-minute time-use interval, with a minimum of an hour between two notifications. Respondents had ten minutes to answer these questions, otherwise the experience sample was recorded as a missing.

Table 3.4 shows the number of responses to the ESM questions for both fieldwork days of the second pilot. It is striking that a rather low number of participants in the pilot completed all seven mood questions received. It was much more common for people to respond only to some questions. This might be because they did not notice all pop-ups, or were not able to use their smartphone during particular activities (e.g. while playing sport, being in a work meeting, seeing the doctor, driving a car, etc). As the questions disappeared from the screen after ten minutes, it is indeed very likely that people are not always able to answer them within the requested (random) ten-minute interval.

Comparing the groups of participants, it can be seen that smartphone owners have a slightly higher number of completed mood questions compared to the inexperienced users. One reason for this may be that for smartphone owners their mobile phone is a more integrated part of their lives, so that they paid more attention to the notifications that appeared on the screen compared to the inexperienced smartphone users, who may not be (or less) familiar with these kinds of pop-ups.

Table 3.4
Response to seven ESM questions

Day	Completed	Smartphone owners	Inexperienced users
Wednesday	7 total	5	0
	3-6 total	21	5
	1-3 total	18	16
	0	4	12
Saturday	7 total	2	1
	3-6 total	15	8
	1-3 total	10	9
	0	2	6

Source: SCP/CentERdata(STBO'11/'12-pilot)

In the third pilot wave, the same subjects were asked to participate one final time on a Wednesday and a Saturday in May 2012 (see Table 3.1 for the exact fieldwork dates). For this test, the app was updated to provide better technical support. Additionally, we implemented the possibility for respondents to enter activities in their own words if they could not find a suitable category in the list provided within the app. This function was implemented in such a way that after typing in the activity, the respondent received a list of the possible categories, so that they could select the appropriate one. If an activity was entered that did not match any of the pre-set categories, it was added to the respondent's list of activity categories from which they could choose in the future.

Additionally, we experimented in this wave with collecting log-data of people's communication behaviour on their own smartphone, in the form of the frequency with which people called and sent text messages (SMS). Only metadata about the frequency of this communication behaviour was logged, not the actual content of the calls and messages, nor the phone numbers which were contacted.

Pilot 4
In addition to testing the app for Android phones, a fourth pilot test was conducted among persons owning an iPhone. To this end, the design of the app developed for the Android system was 'translated' to the iOS-format, the operating system used on the iPhone. To test this app, 50 iPhone users were selected to participate on a weekday

(Wednesday) and weekend day (Saturday). The aim was to test whether the app was also suitable for this type of smartphone, both technically and in terms of user-friendliness. This group of iPhone users did not differ in terms of background characteristics from those selected for the pilot test with the Android smartphones and the borrowed phones (Table 3.5). This is important, as it enables the data quality of the different groups selected to be compared whilst keeping the basic background characteristics stable. As can be seen from Table 3.6, rather high completion rates were obtained for the iPhone users on both fieldwork days.

Table 3.5
Demographics for iPhone participants in Pilot 4 (June 2012)

	Smartphone owners (iPhone)
Gender: Male	24
Female	21
Age	41.0 years
Education: high	28
middle	12
low	5

Source: scp/CentERdata(stbo'11/'12-pilot)

Table 3.6
Response numbers of Pilot 4 (June 2012)

Day 1: Wednesday	Smartphone owners (iPhone)
Complete	43
Partially complete	3
No observations	1
Never logged in	3
Day 2: Saturday	
Complete	46
Partially complete	1
No observations	0
Never logged in	3

Source: scp/CentERdata(stbo'11/'12-pilot)

Evaluation interviews
In order to evaluate the usability of the time use app for both experienced and inexperienced smartphone users, following the first pilot test all respondents received an online evaluation questionnaire. Subsequently, qualitative in-depth interviews were conducted

with nine participants between 13 and 16 March 2012. These respondents were selected based on the type of telephone they used during the first pilot (four with their own smartphone and five with a borrowed one), the type of problems reported in the evaluation questionnaire (three persons were selected who reported no problems, three who reported problems related to time registration and three who had difficulties with the activity selection) as well as gender (six females and three males). Their ages ranged from 31 to 64 years. A third of the selected respondents were interviewed face-to-face and two-thirds by telephone. TNS Nipo conducted the interviews, following a predetermined document prepared by CentERdata and SCP containing the items to be discussed. Researchers from both institutes were also present during the interviews, thus enabling direct interaction with the interviewer if necessary (e.g. to ask about particular issues in more detail).

Note

1   The Longitudinal Internet Studies for the Social sciences (LISS) panel is administered by CentERdata and is an online panel based on a probability sample of households in the Netherlands. It is not an online access panel, as respondents cannot select themselves to participate in research. Instead, the panel is based on a probability sample of households drawn from the population register by Statistics Netherlands. Households that could not otherwise participate are provided with a computer and Internet connection by CentERdata. The panel consists of 5,000 households, comprising 8,000 persons. For more information about the LISS panel, see www.lissdata.nl

4   Results

Although the data collected in the four experimental pilot waves (about 150 participants) are not extensive enough to enable in-depth quantitative analyses to be performed, some indications can be provided about the quality of the time use data collected through the smartphone app. Information can also be gained about the additional data collected through the experience sampling (i.e. beeper) method and reality mining functionalities (GPS tracker). This auxiliary information can be related to the time use data recorded in the diary app and can provide a more detailed overview of the time spent on activities, how people felt and where they were.

In total, 150 respondents were selected to participate in the successive pilot waves. They formed three different groups of smartphone users: about 50 persons without a smartphone, 50 owners of an Android smartphone and 50 iPhone users. In the analyses, we will focus on the comparison between the smartphone owners (Android or iPhone) and inexperienced users (who borrowed a smartphone), rather than between the subjects of the pilot study and the respondents in the traditional time use survey which was conducted in the Netherlands between March 2011 and March 2012. That comparison in methodological and substantive terms will be performed in the next stage of the study, when the results of the main survey are collected (September 2012-2013); see Section 6 for more information.

An important limitation of the relatively low number of respondents in the pilot study concerns the possible impact on the results, or bias, due to extreme scores from one person. The reader should bear this in mind when interpreting the results presented.

4.1   Data quality

There are large differences in the way time use data of respondents are recorded between the regular Dutch time use study, using a paper diary, and when using a smartphone. Additionally, the quality of data from different groups of smartphones users may vary. More generally, differences in data quality can be assessed by evaluating the number of recorded episodes, the number of side-activities and the number of missing main activities (see for references Kamphuis et al. 2009; United Nations 2005).

The first way of checking data quality is to count how many different episodes people report. An episode is defined as a continuous time period in which a respondent does the same activity (and side-activity) with the same person(s) or alone (e.g. 'partner leaves room while watching TV' is a new episode). The general assumption is that the more episodes people report, the higher the data quality will be (in terms of greater accuracy of the reported time use data).

In order to have some indication, we compared the number of episodes recorded during the first smartphone pilot with previous time use studies in the Netherlands (TBO2005, TBO2006). We cannot compare the studies in methodological detail, as the number of possible categories for each study (see Table 4.1) will have a direct effect on the number of possible episodes. However, we think it could give a general indication of the 'usual' number of episodes to be expected in this kind of time use research. It also provides us an idea of how accurately the time use data were recorded by the respondents in the smartphone app.

Data are presented from the first pilot wave, as this may correspond most closely to a survey in which people only participate once (rather than using data from the successive waves, in which learning effects may occur as people had participated in the same research previously). The three studies presented differ in the way in which the data were collected (see Table 4.1, and Appendix A for more details). Firstly, in TBO2005 the time interval to record activities in the diary was 15 minutes rather than the ten minutes required by the HETUS guidelines. Secondly, in the time use studies TBO2005 and TBO2006, more activity categories were distinguished than in the smartphone survey, for which a condensed list was preferred that could fit on the smartphone screen (or at least could be scrolled easily). In TBO2005 and the smartphone pilot, the coding was closed, whereas in TBO2006 people could describe their activities in their own words. These differences probably have an effect on the number of episodes people (can) report. Based on these methodological differences we might expect the number of episodes reported (thus performing a similar activity for a certain period of time) to be lower in the smartphone survey, as only 39 categories were used instead of 260 and 360, respectively, in the traditional Dutch time use surveys from 2005 and 2006.[1]

Table 4.1
Survey characteristics that may affect data quality

	TBO2005	TBO2006	Smartphone2011
Time interval	15 minutes	10 minutes	10 minutes
Number of categories	260	360	39
Type of coding	CLOSED	OPEN	CLOSED

Source: SCP/CentERdata(STBO'11/'12-pilot)

Figure 4.1 shows that for all three studies, the number of episodes is lower on a Saturday than on a Wednesday. The overall pattern of reporting episodes in the smartphone app on different days thus seems to be in line with other, more traditional time use research. With about 27 episodes recorded in the smartphone experiment, the number is in between the TBO2005 and TBO2006 studies (which were respectively based on closed and open coding and a much higher number of categories). This seems to indicate that the number of episodes reported using the smartphone app do not differ substantially from that in similar time use research. This also implies that the number of episodes reported was not much lower in the smartphone diary compared to the traditional time use surveys. On the contrary, even with this relatively low number of activity categories in the smartphone diary (39), the number of episodes recorded is higher than in the 2005 Dutch time use survey which used 260 categories (though used slightly longer time-use intervals). [2]

Overall, differences observed could be due to several reasons, which we cannot explore further here. Differences might be an indication of higher data quality, but might also be due to differences in coding (open or closed), the number of categories used to code the activities reported (39 in the smartphone pilot versus 260 in the Dutch 2005 time use survey) or the length of the time intervals used in the diary (15 or 10 minutes). The fact that the number of episodes reported in the smartphone pilot lies between the two traditional time use studies might indicate that the data quality is not substantially different from that in similar studies. Indeed, even with the closed and rather limited number of categories available (compared to both other time use studies), the number of reported episodes is generally in line with earlier findings.

Figure 4.2 presents the differences in the number of episodes recorded by respondents participating with a borrowed smartphone or their own device. In particular, it can be seen that the number of episodes is somewhat higher among respondents with a borrowed phone compared with respondents using their own phone. Differences between Android and iPhone users are smaller. It might be the case that persons with a borrowed telephone feel more obliged to do a good job using the time-use app, and therefore complete their diary more accurately (i.e. by recording more episodes) than participants with their own smartphone.

The differences observed in Figure 4.2 can mainly be attributed to differences in the participation by people with their own or a borrowed smartphone, as basic background characteristics (i.e. age, gender and education) were kept similar for the three groups (Android owners, iPhone owners and inexperienced users) at the selection stage. Analysing other background characteristics that might affect the results, or analysing these in a multivariate approach, might not provide highly robust findings, because of the limited number of subjects in each group (about 50).

Figure 4.1

Number of episodes on weekday and weekend day, compared between the first smartphone pilot (2011) and the Dutch time use surveys (TBO) in 2005 and (TBO) in 2006

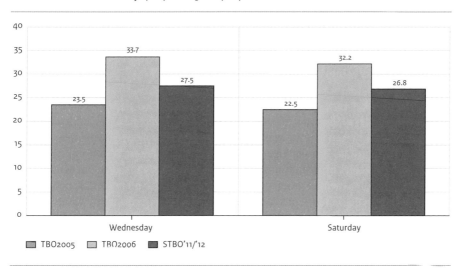

Source: SCP/CentERdata (STBO'11/'12-pilot)

Figure 4.2

Number of episodes on weekday and weekend day, compared between three groups of smartphone users (Pilot 1 and Pilot 4)

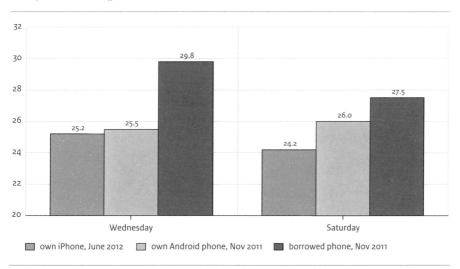

Source: SCP/CentERdata (STBO'11/'12-pilot)

Additionally, the number of activities that people typed in their own words might give an indication of how the categories used in the smartphone app corresponded with the activities in people's minds. For the second pilot, in which people were able to type activities in their own words in addition to the category list used, about 10% of all the activities recorded were entered in this way. Drinking coffee is mentioned especially frequently by respondents as an additional activity not readily found in the category list. This might be because people could see this as drinking, chatting or a break from work, all of which are different activities in the category list.

Figure 4.3 shows the time points at which respondents recorded activities in their diary app for the first day of fieldwork (Pilot 1). As might be expected, most respondents fill in their diary at times when they are most likely to be awake, i.e. between approximately 6.00 a.m. and 1.00 a.m. (see also Figure 4.4). The peak moment for recording activities in the diary is at 8 o'clock in the morning, which corresponds to the moment when the first reminder of the day is sent to respondents, reminding them to fill in their diary. Such a reminder thus seems to have a marked effect on completing the diary. The observation that respondents recorded their activities frequently throughout the day may also be partly due to the use of reminders. These were sent to respondents if there was no diary activity during the preceding two hours. It also seems that people very often complete their diary just before going to bed, at around 10 o'clock in the evening. On average, people fill in their diary eleven times a day, with 207 minutes (roughly three and a half hours) between the updates. A slight difference can be observed in how often participants with and without their own smartphone recorded activities in the diary: smartphone owners recorded their time use about ten times a day, while people with a borrowed smartphone did so on average 12.5 times a day. This may be related to the above observation that those with a borrowed smartphone seemed to be more eager to fill in the diary and also reported more episodes.

Figure 4.3
Time points at which people updated their diary (Wednesday; Pilot 1)

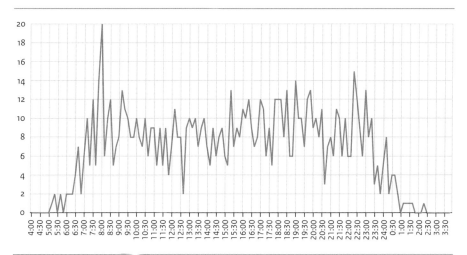

Source: SCP/CentERdata (STBO'11/'12-pilot)

To have some indication of the validity of the substantive results obtained by the smart-phone diary, we can evaluate whether the patterns observed by the smartphone app resemble those from similar time use research. To this end, Figures 4.4 and 4.5 provide an overview of the times at which people sleep and eat on Wednesday and Saturday. These behaviours can be considered fairly stable over time and hence might be a good reference point for providing some indication of the validity of the time use results. We do indeed observe time use patterns for sleeping and eating which are highly similar to previous time use research conducted (on a weekday and weekend day) in the Netherlands since 1975 (see Appendix D). Although the first pilot wave only contained about 100 respond-ents (and therefore the substantive results cannot be compared in detail with other diary-based studies), it is striking that the patterns observed for sleeping and eating by the smartphone diary do not deviate much from the overall patterns found in previous time use studies.

Figure 4.4

Percentage of people sleeping on a day, for Wednesday and Saturday (Pilot 1)

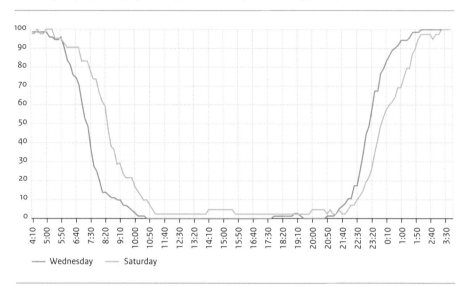

Source: scp/CentERdata (stbo'11/'12-pilot)

Figure 4.5

Percentage of people eating on a day, for Wednesday and Saturday (Pilot 1)

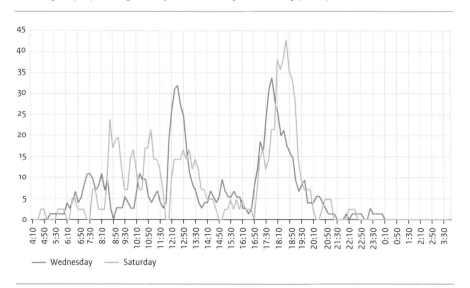

Source: scp/CentERdata (stbo'11/'12-pilot)

Overall, it seems that there are some differences between the data collected by the traditional paper diary and the smartphone app, but that there are at first glance no major deviations. Particularly interesting to note is that the inexperienced smartphone users also show good data quality, even performing slightly better in terms of the number of episodes and frequency of updates recorded in the diary compared to the smartphone owners.

4.2 Reality mining illustrated

During the pilot tests, we used reality mining to explore the possibility of tracking people's locations using the GPS facility on their smartphone, instead of asking them about all the different locations they visited during the day. To enable this, people gave explicit permission before downloading the app. In addition, participants could turn off the GPS tracking on their smartphone at any time during the research.

On the first fieldwork day (Wednesday; Pilot 1) 24,394 GPS location points were collected for 82 respondents. This is a great bulk of data to be analyzed, especially if more respondents were involved in larger surveys and more days were considered. Another observation is that the number of location points differs greatly between the respondents, ranging from one to 2,706 locations stored per day. The average number of location points tracked is 297, with a median value of 35. The majority of all location points was collected by GPS information (90.8%), the other 9.2% through network information (the latter was used if GPS was not accessible at a particular location).

To illustrate what kind of information can be derived from the GPS location points, Figure 4.6 shows a map with the movements of a respondent.

Figure 4.6

An example of the mobility pattern of a respondent for three days

Source: scp/CentERdata (stbo'11/'12-pilot)

Maps like this may become unreadable if they are created for all respondents, but they can show some overall patterns of mobility at a more aggregated level. For example, the information can be used to study people's travel distances on a given day for work, childcare, leisure activities (such as visiting sports facilities or cultural events). In that case, privacy may also become less of an issue, as only data at an aggregate level are used for research purposes.

In addition to the GPS locations, another form of auxiliary data that we collected from the smartphones was people's communication behaviour using the mobile phone. More specifically, in the third pilot, log-data from people's own (Android) smartphones concerning the frequency of calls and text messages sent were automatically collected by the app. This information makes it possible to give an overview of the communication patterns of respondents' mobile phone use. This is especially interesting because short phone calls and text messages are mostly not covered in the ten-minute intervals of a time diary. Table 4.2 gives an overview of the mean number of placed, received and missed calls, as well as the average number of sent and received messages. Keeping in mind that this is only a small group of respondents, namely those with their own Android phone in Pilot 3 (Wednesday n=28 and Saturday n=24), these numbers should be interpreted very carefully, particularly as one outlier can bias these average numbers. The average number of instances of mobile phone use for calls and text messages are low overall, less than one a day, a little higher for Wednesday in calling behaviour. For future research it might be possible to record more information on the timing and duration of these kinds of activity, or even to log the mobile use of the web browser, app use and other activities (see e.g. Bouwman et al. 2013).

Table 4.2
Average number of incoming and outgoing calls and text messages (Pilot 3)

	incoming calls	outgoing calls	missed calls	incoming messages	outgoing messages
Wednesday	0.6	1.2	0.4	0.7	0.5
Saturday	0.3	0.8	0.1	0.7	0.5
Total	0.5	1.0	0.3	0.7	0.5

Source: scp/CentERdata(stbo'11/'12-pilot)

The advantage of automatically logging communication behaviour in this way is that it can replace survey questions and might be more accurate than when people have to give a self-reported estimate of their behaviour. The downside remains the issue of privacy. Although the content of the communication is not tracked, people might experience even the recording of such metadata as a privacy violation.

4.3 Experience Sampling Method illustrated

In addition to the diary app and GPS tracking, the second pilot included experience sampling questions which popped up on the respondent's smartphone screen seven times during the day. Three different questions were asked each time about how happy, rushed and tired respondents felt at that particular moment. People could indicate on a slider how they felt, ranging from 'not at all' to 'extremely' (happy, rushed, tired). The responses were subsequently coded from 0 (not at all) to 100 (extremely), though people could not see these values on the slider.

A total of 83 respondents participated in the ESM; they received a total of 800 pop-up questions during the two fieldwork days. On the Wednesday, people responded to 252 of the pop-up questions, and to 196 on the Saturday. Participants thus replied to 448 of the total number of pop-up questions sent. This corresponds to a 'response rate' of 56% of all the pop-up questions. Looking at the mean scores of the mood questions, Table 4.3 not surprisingly shows that people tend to be more happy, less rushed and less tired on a Saturday compared to a Wednesday. Furthermore, Figure 4.7 shows that feelings of happiness increase during the day, as well as tiredness for both days. However, the degree to which people feel rushed declines on the weekday but stays roughly the same during the weekend.

Table 4.3
Average ESM scores (on a 0-100-scale; Pilot 2)

	Happy	Rushed	Tired
Wednesday	63	21	35
Saturday	74	11	27
Total	68	17	32

Source: SCP/CentERdata(STBO'11/'12-pilot)

Figure 4.7
Experience sampling results on a weekday and weekend day; by time of day

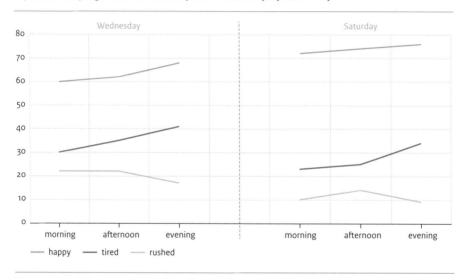

Note: morning is from 8.00 to 12.00 hrs, afternoon from 12.00 to 18.00 hrs and evening from 18.00 to 22.00 hrs
Source: SCP/CentERdata (STBO'11/'12-pilot)

In addition to the pop-up mood questions during the day, respondents could evaluate their day at the end of each fieldwork day. These evaluation questions were about whether people had felt rushed that day, whether it had been a normal or special day and whether they would like more days to be similar to this one. In line with the ESM mood questions, Table 4.4 shows that people evaluate the Saturday more positively (almost three-quarters would like to have more days similar to this one) than the Wednesday. The evaluation question about feeling rushed also shows similar results with the ESM questions, although these scores seem to be a little less extreme compared to the ESM questions about feeling rushed. There seems to be no difference between a weekday and a weekend day in whether or not a day was considered as normal.

Table 4.4
Evaluation day questions (Pilot 2)

	Felt rushed today (answered yes)	Considered the day as not a normal one	Would like to have more days similar to this one (answered yes)
Wednesday (n=84)	14 (17%)	19 (23%)	49 (58%)
Saturday (n=72)	7 (10%)	19 (26%)	52 (72%)
Total (n=156)	21 (14%)	38 (24%)	101 (65%)

Source: scp/CentERdata(stbo'11/'12-pilot)

In general, the pop-up questions about moods during the day, as well as the evaluation questions at the end of the fieldwork day seem to show comparable results. However, the ESM questions allow more detail to be observed about mood fluctuations throughout the day. Furthermore, thanks to the mode of sending questions at random moments during the day, the results of these ESM questions can be considered as reflecting (almost) real-time feelings. People had (at most) ten minutes to respond. For the general evaluation question at the end of the fieldwork day (which was completed at the latest on the day after the fieldwork day) it is not known whether people give a report of their actual feelings, or of the last mood felt at the end of the day, or whether they averaged out their moods of the previous day (which may result in less extreme scores and might tend more to the middle of the mood spectrum). Further investigation of the ESM questions could provide more insight into the fluctuations and the 'actual' feelings. Another possibility is to link the ESM questions to the type of activities people reported in the diary app. This provides an insight into the question as to during which activities in particular people felt more (or less) happy, rushed and tired. This can be analyzed using multi-level methods (using the respondents as the upper 'level' for which several ESM scores were collected). Finally, the ESM questions during the day can be linked to the evaluation survey question at the end of the fieldwork day (at the individual level), which can provide more information about the correlation between these different types of question about the same topic.

4.4 Usability evaluation

To evaluate the usability of the smartphone app for the participants, an evaluation survey was first conducted using an online questionnaire and subsequently in-depth interviews were carried out face-to-face or by telephone.

Evaluation questionnaire

Overall, the results of the evaluation survey showed that respondents did not consider the time use app difficult to use (Table 4.5). Although the number of respondents was quite small, and in particular the number of people who experienced difficulties, some findings are interesting to mention. A frequently reported problem for both smartphone owners and inexperienced users was that the time interval of ten minutes was considered too short. However, this is a general HETUS guideline for time use surveys. Smartphone owners had more problems in finding a suitable category for their activities compared to the inexperienced users, whereas inexperienced users had more difficulties in changing their activities in the day overview. The installation of the app was one of the easiest tasks, even for the inexperienced smartphone users.

Table 4.5
Evaluation questionnaire (response after Pilot 1)

How difficult was it to: (Easy, Neutral, Difficult)	Smartphone owners Difficult	Inexperienced users Difficult
Install + launch app	2%	6%
Fill in activities per 10 min	17%	14%
Use the time wheel for long activities (sleeping & working)	8%	11%
Find a suitable activity category	13%	4%
Indicate with whom an activity was performed	13%	9%
Go back to day overview	6%	11%
Change an activity in day overview	4%	16%
Fill in day questions	8%	4%

Source: SCP/CentERdata(STBO'11/'12-pilot)

The video which demonstrated the use of the smartphone for time use research was evaluated as particularly helpful by most of the respondents (not shown). For example, almost 70% of the inexperienced users found the video helpful for using the app or recording activities (68% and 69%, respectively), compared with 58% and 53% among the smartphone owners. Additionally, 66% of the inexperienced users evaluated the video as helpful for using the (borrowed) smartphone. As might be expected, the figure was much lower for smartphone owners (30%).

In-depth interviews
The results from this evaluation questionnaire induced us to conduct qualitative in-depth interviews with some of the respondents (n=9). Similar to the questionnaire findings, the in-depth interviews showed that the app was easy to use and people really enjoyed participating in this type of research using smartphones to record their time use. The app was intuitive to use, which increased the positive feelings about the overall usability. Respondents completed their diary at several moments during the day, ranging from four times a day to several times per hour. Especially those who performed a lot of activities on a day recorded these more often, as they were afraid of forgetting activities afterwards. Most respondents had consulted the written instructions and the instruction video, though some felt these were unnecessary as they considered themselves capable enough

to use apps. In general, the interviews did not reveal major differences between the experienced and inexperienced smartphone users. It seemed that those who borrowed a smartphone had some previous experience with using such devices. Some issues encountered during the interviews are discussed in more detail below.

Technical problems
First of all, respondents reported technical problems during the first pilot phase, in particular problems with data synchronization. When this occurred, people contacted the helpdesk or visited the website for more information, which helped solve their problems. Some respondents experienced problems with the pop-up questions, in that their telephone screen went black or the telephone stopped working after receiving them. Also, the prepaid credit on the borrowed smartphones expired very quickly in some cases. It turned out that due to technical problems with the data synchronization in the first stages of the pilot, the borrowed smartphones were trying to connect with the server at times when no free Internet connection was available (i.e. through 3G).

The problems in relation to data synchronization were solved by the software developers for the later pilot waves. Also, instead of prepaid smartphones, subscriptions with continuous credit were used for the main survey following the pilot (see Section 6).

Time registration
The use of ten-minute intervals was a frequently cited criticism. For long-term activities this interval was considered too short, while for shorter activities it was felt to be too long. For sleeping and eating we already incorporated another method to record time spent on these activities, in the form of a time wheel. However, this option was not always noticed by respondents, despite being shown in the video manual. In particular, those with a borrowed smartphone did not use the time wheel, while experienced smartphone users seemed to be more accustomed to this functionality. For those who did not notice the time wheel, there was still the possibility of recording time use by copying the previous ten-minute interval. Although this took longer, respondents reported that this also worked perfectly well.

Activity selection
No major problems were reported with selecting the activities in the app. Some respondents experienced difficulties while searching for the pre-set category that most accurately described their activity, but once they were used to the pre-set list of activities, they were able to complete their diary easily. If people could not find a suitable category or were unsure about where to place their activity, they typed it in their own words.
Some people wanted to record their activities in great detail as they considered it important for the research. Therefore, they sometimes wished to have more detailed categories (such as a further breakdown of the category 'culture' into classical and pop culture, or a further distinction within the category 'eating and drinking').

Several tools were provided to help in the selection of activities. Firstly, an information button was visible within the app which contained more information about the activities as well as some examples. Additionally, a written list with the definitions of all activities was provided. Most respondents used one of these help tools to record their activities. Some did not need additional information, as they found the tree structure in the activity list to be clear and obvious.

Two tasks of the diary registration were less clear: listing side-activities and recording who the respondent was with during the activities. Firstly, some of the respondents were not aware that they could list side-activities, as the layout of the app did not show this option very clearly. Secondly, the question about who the respondent was with during the activities was often misinterpreted as meaning who they performed the activity with (e.g. people were cooking alone, but at the same time they were watching television with a partner).

As respondents used the open category to describe activities they could not find in the category list, it is felt to be important to retain this option in addition to a pre-set list of activities. Also, the provision of additional information about activities (within the app and in a written manual) proved to be important help tools for respondents.

As the main purpose of the smartphone study was to be as similar as possible to the traditional time use surveys conducted in the Netherlands following the HETUS guidelines, we maintained the original 'with whom' question, which is identical to the regular time use survey. In that survey, too, this question can be misinterpreted by some respondents. Thus, for reasons of comparability we continued using the same question. In the written manual and information button within the app, a definition of this question was provided (i.e. the respondent was in the same room with someone else during the time of the activity, but not necessarily performing the same activity).

Pop-up questions
The mood questions which popped up on the telephone screen at random moments during the day were considered clear and straightforward to answer. Respondents reported that they answered these short questions based on their feelings at that particular moment, which is the precise intention of this kind of pop-up survey questions. However, at the same time, people felt that these questions often popped up at an inconvenient moment. Since the notification of the mood questions made a sound (ringing, beeping or buzzing), this was experienced as annoying by several respondents. If participants wished not to be bothered for a while (e.g. during a classical music concert or a meeting at work), they could of course always turn off their smartphone, which resulted in a lower number of pop-up questions that could be answered. The implication for future research is that a good balance is important between obtaining high response rates on these pop-up questions (i.e. by notifying people that a new question has just popped up which they need to answer) and people's ability to answer every beep of the smartphone app (and their possibly negative feelings associated with receiving beeps at inconvenient times).

GPS tracking

Finally, the question about allowing the collection of location details by GPS before installing the app was not always noticed by the respondents. Although some respondents had the GPS tracker on their smartphone turned off at all times, most had it turned on. A few people reported that due to the GPS function the telephone battery discharged more quickly than normal. When asked explicitly in the in-depth interview, none of the respondents said they would refuse the collection of location information by GPS tracking for this type of time use research. Thus, privacy was not considered a major problem by the respondents interviewed.

Notes

1   In the first pilot wave, 39 predetermined categories of activities were used. Based on the experiences during this first wave, two additional categories were added, namely `Online banking and online shopping' and `Registering time use by the smartphone'. In the subsequent waves of the pilot, a list with 41 activity categories was used (see also Appendix A).

2   A next step which will be performed based on the consecutive main survey data is to collapse the number of categories in each of the studies to the 41 categories used in the smartphone app. For this pilot, however, this was not done yet (as decisions need to be made for each of the 360 and 260 categories of the respectively 2005- and 2006-time use studies how to collapse them into the 41 activity categories, and for some detailed categories the Dutch time use studies deviate somewhat from the HETUS-classifications).

5 Conclusion and discussion

The number of people using mobile devices to access the Web is growing; in 2012 about 60% of the Dutch population accessed the Internet using a mobile phone (CBS Statline 2013). Smartphones will become a more important and more integrated part of people's everyday lives in the future. The new way of using telephones in day-to-day life can open the way to a new method of data collection, in a way which is comparable to the development of the Internet as a new means of data collection during the last two decades. It will create opportunities for survey research on new domains and topics, and at the same time will introduce changes in the implementation of online and mobile surveys.

Positive evaluation of technical feasibility: smartphones can be used

Based on the series of pilots that we conducted, we can answer our first research question positively: it is feasible to conduct (time use) research using an app on a smartphone for both experienced and inexperienced users. Respondents are able to use the app as a tool to record their time use in a mobile diary and indications were found that the data quality is in line with previous time use studies. Some participants reported problems with finding the relevant activities or considered the time intervals to be too short, but the majority of the respondents were positive about the smartphone study and the usability of the survey-app. Some differences were observed in recording time use between smartphone owners and inexperienced users. Inexperienced users reported more episodes during the day and updated their diary more often than the smartphone owners, implying better data quality. One possible explanation for this might be that those with a borrowed smartphone felt obliged to fill in their diary very accurately, which resulted in slightly more episodes being reported. On the other hand, smartphone owners responded to more of the questions in the ESM (Experience Sampling Method) or beeper-method. This might be related to the natural way in which people use their smartphones: if something pops up on the telephone screen, experienced smartphone users notice this and act upon it (i.e. responding to a question, in the same way as responding to an incoming message via SMS, What's app, Facebook Chat, etc).

The information obtained from the pop-up mood questions and the reality mining (GPS and log-data) can provide social researchers with more insight than when relying solely on survey questions or diary information. For example, it was observed that the random pop-up questions showed actual fluctuations in moods during the day, which cannot be seen based on a general estimation at the end of a fieldwork day (which is often not reported until the following day). This indicates that the short questions which popped up on the telephone screen several times a day more accurately reflect people's real-time feelings. It therefore seems feasible to incorporate this kind of method in smartphone surveys, as it provides additional information (second research question). Also, the reality mining possibilities showed that data complementary to a survey questionnaire (auxiliary data) can be collected through smartphones, for which respondents do not need to take additional action (third research question). Although such reality mining possibilities are endless, it should be noted that there are also limitations, due to technology and privacy. The privacy issue is discussed in more detail below. Technically, it is possible to collect all kinds of additional data from respondents, but the volume of data obtained also poses new challenges for survey researchers (as datasets may become too large, several data points are collected for each individual, 'traditional' information of averages may not represent the data well, etc). Furthermore, we observed that it is difficult to interpret data that are missing for respondents: was this a substantive 'missing' (e.g. did they not make any calls during the day) or were the data not logged correctly due to technical reasons?

Advantages and disadvantages of smartphone research

In general, respondents evaluated their participation in the time use research using smartphones as very positive. They enjoyed filling in their smartphone diary. This might indicate that using a smartphone app for time use research could improve response rates, which are generally rather low for this kind of research, by using innovative data collection methods. The fact that respondents recorded their activities on average eleven times a day is also an important advantage of time use surveys conducted by smartphone. It seems that people completed their diary during those 'lost' moments throughout the day when they are checking the news, their messages, the latest updates on social networking sites, etc. The fact that people mostly carry their mobile phone with them all day and that people regularly completed the diary might actually result in a more accurate record of people's time use than with more traditional methods, as less recall is necessary afterwards about the activities performed.

The use of reminders may have helped greatly in obtaining relatively high completion (i.e. response) rates in the various pilot waves. For example, a peak in updating the diary was observed at 8.00 a.m., when the first reminder of the day was sent. Using reminders is very easy in the technology of the smartphone app. This app can record when and how often people fill in their diary, and based on this information notifications can be automatically sent to respondents. This may be an important cost-reducing factor for smartphone research compared to more traditional survey methods, in which interviewers sometimes need to visit respondents at home or call them to remind them about filling in the diary.

Another important cost reduction is that people can participate using their own device/and that data are automatically stored in the researcher's database. For the pilot study, the costs incurred were rather high, as smartphones needed to be bought and pre-paid amounts of credit were necessary for the data synchronization. Furthermore, the app (as well as the instruction film) needed to be developed and tested extensively before they could be implemented with actual respondents.

With regard to implementing a smartphone app in future social research, we would high-light in particular two issues which need to be addressed: representativeness due to coverage problems, and privacy related to collecting data from people's personal telephones.

Representativeness

One of the (still major) problems of using smartphones in population studies is representativeness, in the sense that not everybody has access to these devices. Consequently, large coverage and selection biases could occur in studies which are conducted entirely by smartphones and which are intended to be representative for the general population (if no smartphones are provided to non-users). Based on Roger's theory of diffusion (1995; 2003), Huysmans and De Haan (2010) expected that by 2015 an (almost) full adoption of smartphone technology would be visible among the Dutch public, meaning that everyone would own a smartphone. In particular, lower costs and possibly fewer alternatives to purchasing smartphones might indeed lead to such a full smartphone penetration among the public. However, some counter-arguments might be that there will always be people in the population who will never use a smartphone because they cannot afford it or because they have arguments for not using it (e.g. constant availability and the urge to check social media updates continuously).

In addition to having access to technology (in this case by owning a smartphone), differences in use and skills related to the mobile device might persist. Hargittai (2002) labels such skill differences in addition to access differences as 'the second-level digital divide'. Indications are that while the access gap is closing, the skills gap for new media technology and digital devices is persisting or even widening (Hargittai 2002). Based on our experiences in the pilot study, we should conclude that overall only small differences were observed between the experienced and inexperienced smartphone users, though this was tested among panel members who might be somewhat more experienced with using this kind of technology to respond to surveys. We observed that even those who did not own a smartphone, but borrowed one during the fieldwork period, seemed to be capable of filling in the smartphone diary. As stated earlier, they actually produced higher data quality (in terms of more time episodes reported and more frequent updates recorded in the diary). However, during the qualitative interviews, some more subtle differences could be observed between the inexperienced and experienced smartphone users. For example, those who owned a smartphone were more familiar with applications frequently used in mobile apps, such as the time wheel. The inexperienced users sometimes copied their ten-minute interval for activities which took a long time, such as sleeping or working, while the experienced users just clicked on the beginning and end time of these activities in the time wheel. The result of both actions is identical, but the inexperienced users might have spent more time on recording the same activity. In the pilot, the groups of smartphone owners and inexperienced users were purposefully selected to obtain similar basic background characteristics, so that differences observed could be (mainly) attributed to differences in experience with smartphone use. However, in a representative study, it will be important to take into account the composition of the groups and their background characteristics.

Representativeness was not an issue in the pilot, as its main aims were experimental, though for the implementation of a smartphone survey in the general population (such as in Section 6), the issue of representativeness needs to be addressed. A possible solution is to provide smartphones to respondents who do not own one. In this way, possible coverage bias due to having or not having a smartphone can be taken into account, as well as possible differences in the substantive results between experienced and inexperienced smartphone users.

Another option would be to use a mixed mode design in which smartphones are one method in addition to other more traditional survey methods. The great advantage is that this would enable a part of the survey to be conducted at relatively low cost, as people participate with their own device, with which they are probably also familiar and use on a daily basis. A drawback of such a mixed mode design, however, is that mode differences might produce effects on the substantive results that might be difficult to attribute to the mode. Furthermore, in such a design the additional functionalities of smartphones cannot be fully used, as only a (probably selective) part of the sample can be surveyed using pop-up questions or tracked based on their GPS location and log-data from their smartphone.

Privacy

Another important issue related to smartphone surveys is privacy. As with other types of survey, privacy mostly forms part of broader survey guidelines. In the pilot, the fieldwork agency that collected the smartphone data complied with the MOA guidelines for conducting survey research and statistics. Protection of respondents' personal information collected by surveys is an important aspect of these guidelines.[1] Furthermore, our pilot study, in line with other studies (Bouwman et al. 2013), was based on informed consent. Subjects were explicitly informed that their GPS location and communication log-data would be stored and they needed to give their consent for this before the app could be downloaded. Additionally, the GPS tracking could be turned off by the respondent at any time. It was interestingly to note that even if respondents had not noticed that their GPS locations were being recorded, none of them in the in-depth interviews said they would be concerned if their GPS locations were tracked for research purposes. However, it should be noted that this view was expressed by panel members, who might have a more positive attitude towards survey research than the general public. Overall, it is important that even if respondents are concerned about the possibility of their privacy being violated by data collection, researchers remain responsible for protecting against the potential risks of privacy infringement.

If survey questions are indeed replaced in the future by reality mining options or extensive 'big data scraping' from the Web, which might collect data without people even knowing it, privacy might become an increasingly important issue to address, including by social researchers. Moreover, as smartphone research is rather new, people may not yet be fully aware of privacy violations that might be related to this kind of data collection. Public attitudes towards privacy may also be affected (and hence possibly change) by broader social developments. For example, the recent disclosure that the U.S. government tracks people's calls, messages, e-mails and social media use on a worldwide basis might affect public opinion about recording such data, even for research purposes. Although social researchers would record only metadata about the frequency and length of communication behaviour, this might already be considered as a privacy violation. Tracking locations by GPS might also be too personal for some people, even if researchers only use the data at a more aggregate level.

A final note about technology

The pilot showed that smartphones can be used in social research as an innovative method of data collection. However, there is always the risk that due to technological problems, data are not correctly recorded or may even be (partly or completely) missing. Therefore, the occurrence of several technical problems during the first pilot wave leads to the recommendation for similar research to allow enough time for testing, as unforeseen technical problems might always arise. Another recommendation is to conduct some in-depth qualitative interviews with actual respondents. The feedback from users about their own experiences provided very valuable information that may help improve not only smartphone surveys but also time use research in general (as people expressed some confusion about the generally implemented HETUS guidelines for time use surveys). Furthermore, the use of video material as an additional support tool can be recommended, as pictures are worth a thousand words. For inexperienced users, the video instruction illustrated very well how the smartphone and app should be used for the research aims.

Technology is developing so rapidly that it is not clear today what will be possible tomorrow. Already, some experiments are using the camera function of the smartphone (e.g. Opree 2013; the Mappiness app), asking respondents to take pictures of their home and work environment, what they are reading and whatever else they would be willing to share. Standard smartphone photo apps can recognize books and newspapers, national landmarks and (after some training) familiar faces. Other reality mining functions that could be easily implemented are for instance a (supermarket) receipt scanner to keep track of spending, reporting outside temperatures, and a music recognition app recording the kind of music respondents are listening to. This implies that a broad range of reality mining possibilities is available, which can be used in research to replace long survey questionnaires. This can overcome problems with recall and self-reports for which people often need to give their own estimation of their behaviour, competences and so on. However, the main downside of endless technological opportunities is potential privacy violations, which should always be addressed and minimized in all types of social research.

Also the measurement device itself might be subject to rapid changes. Besides smartphones, tablets are also spreading rapidly among the general public. Although people might not always carry their tablets with them, as they do with smartphones, the next generation of 'phablets' or 'PadFones' which integrate smartphones and tablets might yet again change the use of these mobile media in everyday life. Furthermore, when we started to develop the app, this method had great advantages over using online websites accessed by smartphones (because of the long loading time and different layouts on different devices). However, the use of HTML5-based technology might overcome the earlier problems and might become the best cross-platform solution in the near future (Funke 2013). But what will follow next?

Note

1   To address the issue of privacy in the next survey (see Section 6) conducted among the LISS-panel, the strict ethical guidelines of the research institute CentERdata were applied, which ensure (as for each survey) absolute anonymity of the data. Although the data will be publicly available via their website, the exact GPS locations, for example, are shown only at aggregate level, so that the data cannot be traced to a particular person or family. Access to this kind of data is only possible if researchers sign a privacy statement and if the data are stored at CentERdata. It should be noted that ethical approval for questionnaire research among adults is not required in the Netherlands. In general, CentERdata abides by the Dutch Personal Data Protection Act (Wet Bescherming Persoonsgegevens, WBP), which is consistent with and derived from European law (Directive 95/46/EC;. For more information, see <http://europa.eu. int/comm/internal_market/privacy/index_en. htm>).

6   After the pilot... a representative survey

As we can evaluate the pilot study very positively regarding the technical software development and tests, as well as the willingness of respondents to participate, their response quality and the ease with which even inexperienced persons were able to use the smartphone app, we implemented the smartphone app in a larger and representative survey among the Dutch population in 2012/13.

This new smartphone survey which followed the pilot study aims to compare the paper diary of the Dutch time use survey (conducted in 2011/12) to the smartphone diary (data collected in 2012/13) methodologically. Furthermore, based on the combined types of data that can be collected using the smartphone app (time use diary, pop-up questions, telephone log-data), we intend to address research questions about topics such as feelings of time pressure, well-being and happiness. Subjective experiences of health and happiness can for example be related to objective GPS registrations of movements and journeys undertaken. In addition, the detailed diary information can not only be linked to the general survey questions at the end of each day, but also to the mood questions which popped up at several moments during the day. Finally, detailed auxiliary information about mobility and mobile communication is collected by the additional functionalities of smartphones. Mobility issues can be studied based on actual GPS distances travelled for work, childcare and leisure. Mobile communication behaviour is recorded by both log-data (of calls and SMS messages sent) and pop-up questions about the use of social media. As these activities mostly occur briefly but frequently during the day, often while doing other activities, this method might provide information that complements the diary and general survey data. Social media use measured in this way can subsequently be related to the diary activities that people performed while using social media, as well as the mood questions (feeling rushed: having the feeling of being connected always and everywhere might be related to feelings of stress).

For the subsequent main survey, we improved the design of the smartphone app based on the technical and usability experiences during the pilot study. Data are collected from a random selection of the LISS-panel, which is representative for the Dutch public aged 16 years and older. People without a smartphone can borrow one from CentERdata (the research institute which manages the LISS-panel). In order to be as similar as possible to the data collected by the traditional time use survey in the Netherlands (2011/12), data are collected for an entire year (2012/13). In this way, possible seasonal influences on the time use data obtained are minimized. Furthermore, this enables CentERdata to reuse each month the smartphones which were provided to respondents. Data collection started in September 2012. Each month, a different batch of about 170 respondents participates, resulting after 12 months in a total net sample of approximately 2,000 participants.

This will provide a better understanding of differences between experienced and inexperienced smartphone users. It will also be possible to compare the smartphone data collection in more methodological detail with the traditional Dutch time use surveys using a paper diary, both based on the HETUS guidelines. Finally, the representative sample and additional functionalities of the smartphone survey enables us to address additional research questions about various topics (well-being, feelings of time pressure, mobility, social media use, etc). In particular, the combination of the different types of data collected using the smartphones may give us a more refined answer than would ever be possible based on survey questions alone.

References

Abraham, K.G., A. Maitland and S.M. Bianchi (2006). Nonresponse in the American Time Use Survey: Who Is Missing from the Data and How Much Does It Matter? In: *Public Opinion Quarterly*, vol. 70, p. 676-703.

Abraham, K.G., S. Helms and S. Presser (2009). How Social Processes Distort Measurement: The Impact of Survey Nonresponse on Estimates of Volunteer Work in the United States. In: *American Journal of Sociology*, vol. 114, no. 4, p. 1129–1165.

Bohte, W. (2010). *Residential self-selection and travel. The relationship between travel-related attitudes, built environment characteristics and travel behaviour* (PhD Thesis). Delft: Delft University of Technology.

Bouwman, H., N. Heerschap and M. de Reuver (2013). *Mobile handset study 2012: evaluation of mobile measurement software to monitor the use of smartphones and tablets in the Netherlands*. Delft/Den Haag: CBS (Statistics Netherlands) and TUDelft (Delft University of Technology).

Bullock, P., P. Stopher, G. Pointer and Q. Jiang (2003). *Gps measurement of travel times, driving cycles and congestion* (Institute of Transport Studies Working Paper), London: Railtrack PLC.

Buskirk, T.D., M. Gaynor, C. Andrus and C. Gorrell (2011). *An app a day could keep the doctor away: comparing mode effects for a iphone survey related to health app use*. Phoenix, Arizona: American Association of Public Opinion Research.

Buskirk, T.D. and C. Andrus (2012). Smart surveys for smart phones: exploring various approaches for conducting online mobile surveys via Smartphones. In: *Survey Practice*, vol. 5, no. 1 (www.surveypractice.org).

Callegaro, M. (2010). *Do you know which device your respondent has used to take your online survey?* In: *Survey Practice*, December 2010 (www.surveypractice.org).

CBS Statline (2013). *ICT gebruik van personen naar persoonskenmerken*. CBS (Statistics Netherlands). Consulted May 2013 via http://statline.cbs.nl

Cloïn, M. (ed.) (2013). *Tijdsbestedingsonderzoek 2011 rapportage (werktitel)* [Time use survey 2011 report (working title)]. The Hague: the Netherlands Institute for Social Research | SCP.

Couper, M.P. (2010). *Visual design in online surveys: Learnings for the mobile world* (Paper presented at the Mobile Research Conference 2010, London). Consulted November 2011 via http://www.mobileresearchconference.com/uploads/files/MRC2010_Couper_Keynote.pdf

Eurostat (2009). *Harmonized European time use surveys (HETUS), Guidelines 2008* (Methodologies and Working Papers). Luxembourg: Office for Official Publications of the European Communities.

Fuchs, M. and B. Busse (2009). The coverage bias of mobile web surveys across European countries. In: *International Journal of Internet Science*, vol. 4, no. 1, p. 21–33.

Funke, F. (2013). *HTML5 and mobile Web surveys: A Web experiment on new input types* (Paper presented at the General Online Research Conference (GOR), 4-6 March 2013), Mannheim: University Mannheim.

Gershuny, J. and O. Sullivan (1998). The sociological uses of time-use diary analysis. In: *European Sociological Review*, vol. 14, no. 1, p. 69-85.

Hargittai, E. (2002). Second level digital divide: differences in people's online skills. In: *First Monday*, vol. 7, no. 4. Consulted April 2012 via http://firstmonday.org/htbin/cgiwrap/bin/ojs/index.php/fm/article/view/942/864

Huysmans, F. and J. de Haan (2010). *Alle kanalen staan open* [All channels open]. The Hague: the Netherlands Institute for Social Research | SCP.

Kamphuis, C., R. van den Dool, A. van den Broek, I. Stoop, P. Adelaar and J. de Haan (2009). *tbo/eu en tbo/nl. Een vergelijking van twee methoden van tijdsbestedingsonderzoek* [tbo/eu en tbo/nl. A comparison of two methods of time use research]. The Hague: the Netherlands Institute for Social Research | SCP.

Kahneman, D., and A.B. Krueger (2006). Developments in the Measurement of Subjective Well-Being. In: *Journal of Economic Perspectives*, vol. 20, p. 3-24.

Kahneman, D., A.B. Krueger, D. Schkade, N. Schwarz and A. Stone (2004). Toward national well-being accounts. In: *American Economic Review*, vol. 94, p. 429-434.

Killingsworth, M. A., and D.T. Gilbert (2010). A wandering mind is an unhappy mind. In: *Science*, vol. 330, no. 6006, p. 932-932.

Knulst, W., and A. van den Broek (1999). Do Time-use Surveys Succeed in Measuring "Busyness"? Some Observations of the Dutch Case. In: *Loisirs & Société*, vol. 21, no. 2, p. 563-572.

Larson, R., and M. Csikszentmihalyi (1983). The experience sampling method. In: *New Directions for Methodology of Social and Behavioral Science*, vol. 15, p. 41-56

Larson, R. and M.H. Richards (1994). *Divergent realities: the emotional lives of mothers, fathers and adolescents.* New York: Basic Books.

Minnen, J., I. Glorieux, T. P. van Tienoven and D. Weenas (2013). *MOTUS: Modular online Time-Use Survey* (Paper presented at NTTS conference 2013). Brussels: Eurostat.

Opree, S. (2013). *Onderzoek naar mediagebruik van kinderen: experience sampling en dagboekstudies* [Research of media use among children: experience sampling and diary studies] (Paper presented at NPSO-conference 28 May 2013). Amsterdam: KNAW.

Peytchev, A. and C.A. Hill (2010). Experiments in mobile web survey design: Similarities to other modes and unique considerations. In: *Social Science Computer Review*, vol. 28, p.319-335.

PewInternet (2013). *Pew Internet: Mobile. Pew Internet & American life project.* Consulted May 2013 via www.pewinternet.org.

Raento, M., A. Oulasvirta and N. Eagle (2009). Smartphones. An emerging tool for social scientists. In: *Sociological Methods & research*, vol. 37, no. 3, p. 426-454.

Rogers, E. (1995, 2003). *Diffusion of Innovations.* New York: Free Press.

Stopher, P., C. FitzGerald and M. Xu (2007). Assessing the accuracy of the Sydney Household Travel Survey with GPS. In: *Transportation*, vol. 34, p.723-741.

Stoop, I. (2007). No time, too busy. Time strain and survey cooperation. In: G. Loosveldt, M. Swyngedouw and B. Cambré (eds.), *Measuring Meaningful Data in Social Research* (p. 301-314). Leuven: Acco.

Unites Nations (2005). *Guide to producing statistics on time use: measuring paid and unpaid work.* New York: United Nations, Department of Economic and Social Affairs.

Van Ingen, E., I. Stoop and K. Breedveld (2009). Nonresponse in the Dutch Time Use Survey: Strategies for Response Enhancement and Bias Reduction. In: *Field Methods*, vol. 21, no. 1, p. 69-90.

Yen, I.H., C.W. Leung, M. Lan, M. Sarrafzadeh, K.C. Kayekjian and O.K. Duru (2013). A Pilot Study Using Global Positioning Systems (GPS) Devices and Surveys to Ascertain Older Adults. In: *Travel Patterns.* Published online before print March 21, 2013 (doi: 10.1177/0733464813479024).

Appendix

Appendix A Overview of HETUS *guidelines, the Dutch time use survey (*TUS*)* [1] *, and the smartphone app: pilot study and main survey*

HETUS guidelines	Dutch TUS 2011/12	Smartphone TUS	
		Pilot 2011/12	Survey 2012/13
Sample design			
Resident population of the country living in private households, recommendation of 10+ age	Persons living in the Netherlands aged 10 years and older, in private households and entered in the Municipal Personal Records database (GBA)	Persons living in the Netherlands aged 16 years and older, in private households	
Random sample	Stratified two-stage sample of persons entered in the GBA database, stratified by municipality and interview region	Selection of TNS Nipo base panel members, 50% owning a smartphone, 50% without a smartphone	Probability-based selection of LISS panel members, representative of the Dutch population (aged 16+)
Diary days			
At least two diary days: one weekday and one weekend day	Seven successive diary days	Two fixed diary days: Wednesday and Saturday	Two random diary days: one weekday and one weekend day
Coverage of 12-month fieldwork period	Year-round fieldwork, from March 2011 to March 2012	N/A Several waves of tests conducted with the same group of subjects during 2011/12	Year-round fieldwork, from September 2012 to September 2013

(continued)

HETUS guidelines	Dutch TUS 2011/12	Smartphone TUS Pilot 2011/12	Survey 2012/13
Survey forms			
Appropriate method for accompanying questionnaires	Face-to-face in home interviews or by telephone (only for the final questionnaire)	N/A Background (information was known from the panel database)	Online questionnaires (and additional background information was known from the panel database)
Diary method	Self-completed paper diary (PAPI)	Self-completed smartphone diary by mobile app	
Diary			
Fixed ten-minute time slots	Ten minutes	Ten minutes	
Recording of secondary activities, with whom and location	One main + one side-activity, with whom Location surveyed at beginning and end of the day + recording of journeys as activities during the day	One main + one side-activity, with whom Location by GPS + recording of journeys as activities during the day	
Open coding of activities	Open coding, by trained coders	Closed coding, list of predetermined HETUS-categories	
Providing support for respondents	Interviewer makes contact during diary week	Helpdesk for technical and content questions	
Recording of longer activities (sleeping and working)	Every ten minutes, although with whom and side-activities is not needed	No ten-minute interval, wheel for scrolling longer periods, with whom and side-activities not applicable	

Appendix B Hierarchically ordered time use categories in smartphone app *(based on*
HETUS coding; for more information see Eurostat 2009)

CODE	ACTIVITY
V0100	**Sleeping**
	Eating and drinking
V0200	Eating and drinking at home, work or school
V0214	Going out for eating and drinking
V0300	**Personal or medical care**
V1000	**Employment**
	Study/education
V2100	School, university
V2200	Study, course as a hobby
	Domestic work
V3100	Cooking/food preparation
V3200	Household upkeep, cleaning
V3400	Gardening and taking care of pets
V3500	DIY, construction and repairs
V3700	Administration/paper work
	Shopping and services
V3610	Shopping/groceries
V3620	Services
	Caring for/helping children and adults
V3800	Caring and supervising children (of own family)
V3910	Helping other adults within own family
V4200	Helping others outside the family
	Social contacts
V5100	Visits/having visitors, parties
V5110	Having a talk
V5140	Using the telephone
	Television, radio, reading
V8210	Watching television
V8300	Listening to radio and music
V8100	Reading
	Computer and internet
V7230	Gathering information and news via the internet
V7235	Online banking and online shopping
V7240	Communicating through the internet (online)
V7250	Other pc/internet offline
V7330	Computergames

(continued)

CODE	ACTIVITY
	(Other) leisure
V4100	Voluntary work
V6000	Sports
V5250	Visiting sports/competitions
V5210	Going out, cultural visits
V5241	Library
V5260	Trips
V7100	Hobby
V7310	Playing games
V5310	Resting
V4320	Religious and ceremonial activities
	Travelling
V9000_1	Travelling by own means/transport
V9000_2	Travelling by public transport
V9100	Registering time use by the smartphone

Source: scp/CentERdata(stbo'11/'12-pilot)

Appendix C. Invitation letter (in Dutch)

<eigen_aanspreek>
<eigen_straat><eigen_huisnummer>
<eigen_postcodeC><eigen_postcodeL>
<eigen_plaats>

Uw kenmerk   Doorkiesnr. 0---------   E-mail   --@tns-nipo.com
Ons kenmerk --   Datum   16 november 2011

Betreft Deelname tijdsbestedingsonderzoek

Geachte <eigen_aanspreek>,

Deze brief is bedoeld voor <eigen_beoogde>.

Hartelijk dank voor uw deelname aan het tijdsbestedingsonderzoek. Zoals u weet is het doel van dit onderzoek dat u door middel van een applicatie op uw eigen Android smartphone op een aantal dagen uw bezigheden bijhoudt. Voor uw deelname ontvangt u aan het einde van het onderzoek 100 NIPoints.

Voordat u mee kan doen is het van belang dat u deze applicatie op uw telefoon installeert. Op www.centerdata.nl/link/tbonipo kunt u een instructievideo bekijken die laat zien hoe het installeren van de applicatie en invullen op de smartphone werkt. Ook vindt u daar de link naar de applicatie zelf.
Wij raden u aan om deze video een aantal dagen vóór de eerste meetdag alvast te bekijken, de applicatie te installeren en op te starten. Ook adviseren wij dat uw telefoon helemaal is opgeladen voor de start van een meetdag.

Bij het opstarten van de applicatie moet u een inlogcode en een wachtwoord invoeren.
Uw persoonlijke inlogcode en wachtwoord zijn:
Inlogcode: < inlogcode >
Wachtwoord: <wachtwoord>

In eerste instantie zijn er twee meetdagen: woensdag 23 november en zaterdag 26 november. Daarna wordt het verloop van het onderzoek geëvalueerd en zullen er in januari en maart mogelijk nog vier meetdagen zijn.

Z.O.Z.
Enkele dagen voor aanvang van de eerste meetdag krijgt u per e-mail een herinnering, ook krijgt u een SMS op de meetdag zelf.

Tijdens een meetdag is er een helpdesk bereikbaar die u kunt raadplegen bij problemen met het invullen. Voordat u contact opneemt met de helpdesk, verzoeken wij u vriendelijk om eerst de handleiding en de instructievideo goed te bekijken. Het kan zijn dat de oplossing voor uw probleem daarin al gegeven wordt.

De helpdesk kunt u zowel telefonisch (op ---) of per e-mail (---@tns-nipo.com) benaderen. Om snel uw vraag te kunnen afhandelen is het handig als u uw inlogcode bij de hand heeft.

Kort na afloop van de tweede meetdag sturen wij u per e-mail een vragenlijst waarin u uw ervaringen met het onderzoek kunt geven.

Met vriendelijke groet,
TNS NIPO
--

Appendix D. Times at which people sleep and eat on a weekday (Tuesday) and weekend-day (Sunday)[2]

Figure D.1

Times of sleeping on weekday and weekend day

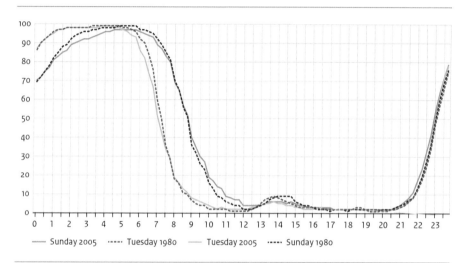

Source: SCP (TBO1980; TBO2005) www.tijdsbesteding.nl

Figure D.2

Times of eating on weekday and weekend day

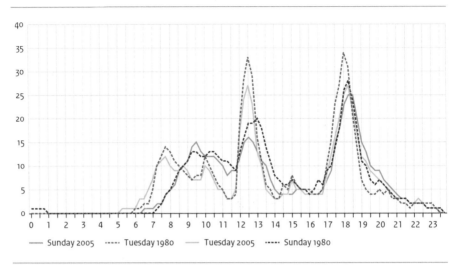

Source: SCP (TBO1980; TBO2005) www.tijdsbesteding.nl

Notes

1   In general, the regular time use survey in the Netherlands follows the HETUS guidelines. However, due to the long tradition (since 1975) of conducting such surveys in the Netherlands, there are some deviations from the general recommendations. First, the HETUS guidelines prescribe the recording of activities on two days for each respondent (a weekday and a weekend day), while the Dutch TUS monitors a whole week (which automatically comprises at least one weekday and one weekend day). The HETUS guidelines also require a household sample in which each individual completes a diary, while the Dutch TUS selects individual persons within private households to complete the diary (HETUS 2009; Kamphuis et al. 2009).

2   More information on the time use patterns in the Netherlands since 1975 for sleeping: http://www.scp.nl/Onderzoek/Tijdsbesteding/Wanneer_en_hoe_laat/Slapen and eating: http://www.scp.nl/Onderzoek/Tijdsbesteding/Wanneer_en_hoe_laat/Eten